Cornerstones of Freedom

The Story of

PRESIDENTIAL ELECTIONS

By Jim Hargrove

D1529514

CHILDRENS PRESS®

CHICAGO

Library of Congress Cataloging-in-Publication Data

Hargrove, Jim.
    The story of presidential elections.

    (Cornerstones of freedom)
    Summary: Examines how presidential elections have
changed over the past 200 years, discussing such topics
as presidential primaries, national conventions,
television campaigns, and funding.
    1.   Presidents—United States—Election—Juvenile
literature.   [1. Presidents—Election]   I.   Title.
II.   Series.
JK528.H37   1988   324.973   88-1021
ISBN 0-516-04737-X

George Washington's Inauguration, April 30, 1789

Ronald Reagan's Inauguration, January 20, 1981

Few events in America are as important—or interesting—as a presidential election. Every four years, millions of U.S. citizens flock to polling places scattered throughout cities, towns, villages, and country crossroads to vote for the next president of the United States. More Americans vote in presidential election years than in any others.

American presidential elections have changed drastically since the Union was established. When the U.S. Constitution was written in 1787, its framers expected only a minority of Americans to vote directly, or even indirectly, in presidential elections.

After calling for presidents and vice presidents to serve four-year terms, the Constitution outlines the election procedure:

> Each State shall appoint, in such Manner as the Legislature thereof may direct, a Number of Electors, equal to the whole Number of Senators and Representatives to which the State may be entitled in the Congress: . . .
>
> The Electors shall meet in their respective States, and vote by Ballot for two Persons, . . . And they shall make a List of all the Persons voted for, and of the Number of Votes for each; which List they shall sign and certify, and transmit sealed to the Seat of the Government of the United States, directed to the President of the Senate. The President of the Senate shall, in the Presence of the Senate and House of Representatives, open all the Certificates, and the Votes shall then be counted. The Person having the greatest Number of Votes shall be the President, if such Number be a Majority of the whole Number of Electors appointed; . . . In every Case, after the Choice of the President, the Person having the greatest Number of Votes of the Electors shall be the Vice President. . .

Without televisions, radios, telephones, and other forms of electronic communication, news traveled slowly in early America. The framers of the Constitution feared that many Americans would not be adequately exposed to the views and abilities of presidential candidates. Therefore, they felt that a small group of well educated and highly respected delegates from each state was best suited to elect a president for the nation.

The Constitution allowed each state legislature to determine how to choose its presidential electors. Some states held general elections, while in others the state legislature directly chose the electors. But even in states holding general elections, many people were not allowed to vote.

In early America, voting requirements in the various states prohibited most or all of the following types of people from voting: women, blacks, Indians, the uneducated, people without property or wealth, as well as those with criminal records or histories of mental illness, and, of course, children. A majority of adults living in early America did not have the right to vote in any government election. Fortunately, nearly every American agreed on who should become the young nation's first president.

On February 4, 1789, sixty-nine Americans, members of the group of presidential electors that be-

When the votes of the 1933 presidential electors were counted, Franklin Delano Roosevelt became the thirty-second president of the United States. FDR was a cousin of Theodore Roosevelt, the twenty-sixth president of the United States.

came known as the Electoral College, voted unanimously for George Washington as America's first president.

But in little more than a decade, the nature of presidential elections changed dramatically. The framers of the Constitution did not anticipate the rise of political parties in American campaigns, but parties arose almost immediately.

The finifhing
STROKE.
Every Shot's a Vote,
and every Vote
KILLS A TORY!
DO YOUR DUTY, REPUBLICANS
Let your exertions this day
Put down the Kings
AND TYRANTS OF BRITAIN.
LAST DAY.
April, 1807.

Supporters of John Adams (right) used anti-
Jefferson posters like the one above to keep
citizens from voting for Jefferson (left).

In 1800, two powerful political parties backed different candidates for president. The Federalists, who supported a strong national government and policies favoring business interests and the wealthy, backed incumbent president John Adams. On the other hand, the Democratic Republicans, favoring the rights of state governments and the common man, supported Thomas Jefferson, author of the Declaration of Independence. America's first presidential election dominated by party politics was as bitter as any in history. Although Adams and Jefferson personally avoided dirty tactics, members of each party savagely attacked their opponents.

In the final days of the year 1800, the votes of the presidential electors from each state were collected and brought to the federal government's new headquarters in Washington, D.C. When the ballots were counted, the Democratic Republican party backing Thomas Jefferson had clearly defeated the Federalist party supporting President John Adams for reelection.

Surprisingly, however, it was still uncertain who would be the president. Democratic Republican electors had cast seventy-three ballots for Thomas Jefferson and an equal number for Aaron Burr, the party's choice for vice president. Although all the electors wanted Jefferson to be president, the Constitution specified that a tied vote had to be decided in the House of Representatives.

Bitter that John Adams had lost the election, many Federalist representatives decided to vote for Burr instead of Jefferson, the obvious choice of the Democratic Republican electors. After dozens of votes taken over a period of nearly a week, neither Jefferson nor Burr could win a clear majority.

On February 17, 1801, the thirty-sixth vote was taken in the House of Representatives. This time, a number of Federalist representatives decided not to vote, thus giving the election to Thomas Jefferson. Aaron Burr became vice president. Three years later, in 1804, the Twelfth Amendment to the Con-

A romanticized view of Washington D.C. about 1800

stitution was ratified. That amendment called for the electors to "name in their ballots the person voted for as President, and in distinct ballots the person voted for as Vice-President. . . ."

The year 1800 was pivotal in the history of American presidential elections. Not only did it prompt the Twelfth Amendment, but also it established the role of a vigorous two-party system in the electoral process.

During the early decades of the 1800s, the right to vote among American males was greatly expanded. Whole new groups of people—including pioneers moving to the new states and territories of the West, as well as industrial workers in the factories of the Northeast—demanded, and soon got, the right to

Andrew Jackson enroute to his inauguration in 1829

vote. About the same time, party politics made it clear that the Electoral College no longer performed the function of careful deliberation intended by the framers of the Constitution. The vote of the presidential electors became little more than a formality, reflecting the choices of the voters from each state (a roll that remains unchanged today).

The common man's power to decide presidential elections was shown in 1828, when Andrew Jackson was elected president. Although he was a military hero, a frontier lawyer, and a U.S. senator, many people regarded Jackson as a commoner. He was the first American president not born to a wealthy land-holding or professional family. But to his supporters he was "the people's president."

During Jackson's two terms in office, another striking change in presidential elections occurred. Until that time, presidential candidates were selected in many different ways, usually involving local politicians, state legislators, and other leaders of political parties. They would sometimes meet in state conventions, large gatherings of the party faithful, during which votes would be taken and a candidate eventually selected. In other cases, candidates would be selected by political caucuses, closed meetings attended by state legislators and important party politicians.

In the late 1820s, a small and now all but forgotten party called the Antimasons was organized to protest the suspicious disappearance of a New Yorker named William Morgan. Morgan was working on a book that would give away secrets of a men's organization known as the Freemasons. All this would have had limited historic importance had the Antimasons not decided to hold national conventions to select political candidates in 1830 and 1831.

As the presidential election of 1832 approached, other political parties also decided to hold national conventions. President Jackson's party held its convention in Baltimore in May 1832. Although the incumbent president had already won renomination in various state conventions and legislative caucuses, the party convention focused attention on

Jackson and his vice presidential running mate, Martin Van Buren. Both men won their elections later that year.

The national conventions of the major political parties soon became traditional.

However, by the beginning of the twentieth century, there was increasing concern about the undemocratic nature of political party conventions. The national conventions were often controlled by a handful of powerful insiders. And although millions of American men could vote in the presidential election in November, they had limited direct input regarding the candidates selected by each of the major parties.

1984 National Democratic Convention

In 1910, the Oregon legislature passed a law calling for statewide presidential primaries. Primaries are much like elections, except that voters choose candidates (or their delegates to political nominating conventions) instead of choosing the actual officeholders themselves. A primary enables a majority of the qualified voters in a state to have a legal voice in the selection of presidential candidates. By the presidential election of 1912, nine other states had followed Oregon's lead and called for presidential primaries.

The changes made in 1912 brought about a heated controversy in the Republican party. Theodore Roosevelt, who had served two terms as president from 1901 to 1909, tried to win the nomination from the incumbent Republican president, William Howard Taft. Roosevelt won nine of the ten state primaries, seemingly proving that he was the overwhelming choice of Republican voters in the United States. But Taft controlled most of the other states, which still used the older and less democratic methods of selecting political candidates.

Finally, it was suggested that Taft and Roosevelt both withdraw from the race and a compromise candidate be selected. "I'll name the compromise candidate," Roosevelt responded. "He'll be me." When Roosevelt lost the Republican nomination to Taft at the national convention, he formed another, or third,

Announcements of Teddy Roosevelt's Bull Moose party (right) even appeared in German publications.

political party, called the Bull Moose party. In the November elections, Roosevelt's Bull Moose party was more successful than Taft's Republican party. But Republican votes were split, resulting in an easy victory for Democratic candidate Woodrow Wilson. (Third parties are rarely successful in American presidential politics, but nevertheless they often influence elections.)

The state primaries of 1912 were unable to win the Republican nomination for Roosevelt, but they did show that primaries were an efficient way to demonstrate popular support for presidential candidates. In subsequent years, an increasing number of states adopted the presidential primary system, growing to thirty-five by 1980, then falling back to twenty-eight in 1984. During the same era, many states still using the caucus system reformed it to reflect more directly the will of the voters.

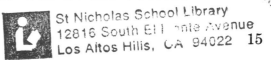
15

In the South, blacks flocked to the polls to exercise their right to vote.

Constitutional and legislative changes over the last hundred years have dramatically increased the number of American citizens qualified to vote in presidential elections. The Fifteenth Amendment to the Constitution, ratified in 1870, made it illegal to deny anyone the right to vote based on color or race. Still, for many years the rights of minority voters, especially blacks, continued to be limited in some states by tactics such as unevenly applied literacy tests and poll taxes.

Of tremendous immediate influence on all forms of elections was the Nineteenth Amendment, ratified in 1920, recognizing the right of women to vote in American elections. The results of the new amendment were clear the very same year. In the presi-

Accompanied by their children, determined women
march for the right to vote in 1912.

dential election of 1916, four years before ratification of the new amendment, 17,667,827 Americans voted for two leading presidential candidates. Four years later in 1920, the figure swelled to 25,299,553. For the first time, a true majority of adult U.S. citizens had the right to vote.

Still other laws have increased the number of Americans eligible to vote in presidential elections. The Twenty-Third Amendment, ratified in 1961, gave residents of Washington, D.C., the previously denied right to vote for presidents and vice presidents. The Twenty-Fourth Amendment, ratified three years later, made it unconstitutional to deny the right to vote to anyone who failed to pay a poll tax or any other tax.

Eighteen year olds register to vote.

In 1965, the U.S. Congress passed a milestone Voting Rights Act, and President Lyndon Johnson signed it into law. The complex regulations basically worked to encourage states to comply more faithfully with the voting rights guaranteed to racial minorities by the Fifteenth Amendment. In 1975, the law was amended to allow persons to vote even if they were unable to read, write, or speak English. And the Twenty-Sixth Amendment to the Constitution, ratified in 1971, gave the right to vote to citizens who had reached their eighteenth birthday.

Clearly, these changes greatly increased the number of U.S. citizens eligible to vote. In 1789, only 69 Americans voted directly in America's first presidential election. Not quite two centuries later, in 1984, the 538 electoral votes that were cast served only to ratify, on a state-by-state basis, the majority will of more than 92 million Americans who voted

Election officials after the polls close

for one of the two major presidential candidates.

The qualifications for becoming a president have remained unchanged since the Constitution was written. A president must be a natural-born U.S. citizen at least thirty-five years of age who has lived in the country at least fourteen years. These, of course, are the minimum requirements. Many presidents have been either lawyers with previous political experience or army generals. So far, thirteen presidents first served as vice president.

Becoming a candidate for president is as easy as making a public announcement. Any American citizen who meets the simple requirements stated in the Constitution can become a legitimate presidential candidate. However, to be a potentially successful candidate seriously considered by large numbers of voters, by the major political parties, and by the news media, is another matter entirely.

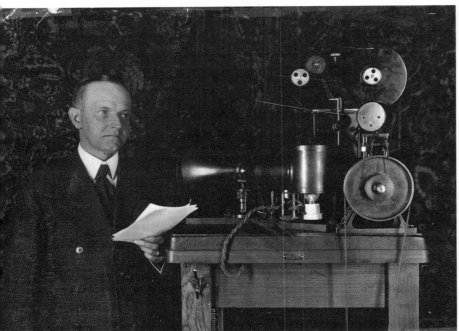

Both Calvin Coolidge (left) and Warren Harding (right) made frequent radio broadcasts to the American people.

People who hold, or have recently held, important political offices usually gain considerable attention once they announce their candidacy. Presidents running for reelection, vice presidents serving retiring presidents, congressional leaders (especially from the Senate), and governors of populous states seem to have the best chances of building strong support for their candidacy. But for them, as well as for lesser-known candidates, the cost of a national campaign presents an urgent need to raise money.

In 1920, a few months before he was elected the twenty-ninth president, Senator Warren G. Harding delivered the first speech carried on radio by a candidate. Following Harding's death three years later, Calvin Coolidge became president and his inaugural address was broadcast over twenty-one radio stations to some fifteen million Americans.

Even though his nickname was "Silent Cal," Coolidge was the first president to extensively use radio. "Silent Cal" even had a radio transmitter installed on his presidential train, so he could broadcast to the American people while he was traveling. About two decades later, Harry Truman became the first president to appear on television. Understanding the growing role of television in American politics, Truman hired a media adviser to help him speak and appear well on television. Immediately, presidential candidates did the same.

Sometimes newspapers falsely predict the outcome of presidential elections. In 1948 the *Chicago Daily Tribune* incorrectly announced that Dewey had defeated Truman. They were wrong—Truman was elected.

Leading up to the presidential election of 1952, won by Dwight Eisenhower, television played—for the first time—a vital role in the campaign process. During his successful 1976 campaign for the presidency, Jimmy Carter used television more than any other candidate before him.

Today, presidential candidates generally spend far more money on television advertisements alone than on radio and print ads combined. They hire consultants to help film both long and short commercials carefully aimed at local, and sometimes national, audiences.

The cost of media and direct-mail advertisements, as well as the expense of traveling and maintaining large campaign organizations, makes it imperative for presidential candidates to raise millions of dollars. According to the League of Women Voters, more than one billion dollars was spent on national, state, and local elections in 1980. About $275 million was spent that year on the presidency alone.

Because such vast sums of money create the potential for abuse, the U.S. Congress passed a law to regulate campaign financing. The Federal Election Campaign Act of 1971, amended a number of times in later years, sets strict rules on how presidential and vice presidential campaign funds can be raised and, in the case of candidates who accept public tax funds, on how they can be spent.

Basically, the complex law allows a candidate to accept no more than one thousand dollars from an individual contributor for each primary or general election the candidate enters. The law also requires candidates to publicly report individual contributions over, most recently, two hundred dollars. Although it details a number of other restrictions, at its simplest, the Federal Election Campaign Act attempts to discourage private citizens or organizations from trying to buy presidential favors from a successful candidate. About the same time Congress passed the original act, it also made available federal grants matching the amount of money a candidate had raised from private contributions, providing the candidate had established campaign committees in at least twenty states.

In recent years, organizations called political action committees (PACs) have flourished because of the restrictions placed on campaign contributions by federal law. PACs are usually started by large corporations, trade unions and associations, and other groups, often with particular points of view. Because of their organization, seldom bound to a single candidate, PACs can make somewhat larger political contributions than private citizens.

More importantly, PACs also can develop media and direct-mail campaigns of their own, with unlimited financing, directed for or against a presidential

President Ronald Reagan and Vice President George Bush at the National Republican Convention

candidate. Ronald Reagan was the first presidential candidate to benefit greatly from the enlarged role of political action committees. In 1980, more than $12 million was spent on private campaigns for Reagan. Incumbent President Jimmy Carter had only $46 thousand worth of independent campaign support, although nearly a quarter million dollars was spent by PACs critical of his presidency.

American presidential elections are far more democratic today than they were in the 1700s, but the campaigns leading up to them are also longer, more complex, and almost unimaginably expensive.

Often the candidates begin their work two years or more before a presidential election. In as many states as possible, they set up campaign organizations, largely staffed by volunteers. The object is twofold: to raise money for the long campaign, and to win delegates to the next national convention of their political party. Winning convention delegates is critical. In all likelihood, the next president of the United States will be someone nominated at the Democratic or Republican national conventions.

Today, states use many different systems to select convention delegates. Some have open primaries, where any registered voter can vote directly for a candidate, or for a delegate who may or may not support a particular candidate. Other states have closed primaries, in which only declared members of a particular political party can vote. Still others adopt proportional systems, in which delegates are appointed according to the portion of the statewide vote won by each candidate on the ballot.

In a few states such as California, the candidate who wins the most votes sometimes gets all the delegates in a "winner-take-all" primary. A number of states also hold nonbinding advisory primaries, sometimes called "presidential beauty contests" because, despite the will of the voters, final selection of candidates is made during closed caucuses. Many states still make use of the caucus system, in which party members vote for representatives who attend a series of local and then statewide meetings, and finally select a candidate.

Presidential candidates spend fortunes campaigning in each state. As soon as one primary or caucus ends, a candidate shifts his major efforts to another state, where another primary or caucus is upcoming. This grueling process usually extends from at least the beginning of the presidential election year until June, when the last primaries or caucuses are held—traditionally in states such as California. During this hectic period, usually some candidates drop out, unable to win sufficient delegates. Still other individuals may announce their candidacy in the middle of this period, hoping that a strong showing in the campaign's final months before the national convention will generate nationwide excitement.

Then sometime during the summer, after all the delegates have been named, the Republicans and the Democrats hold their national conventions.

A keynote address, usually delivered by an important politician in the party, begins the convention. Then delegates turn to the first orders of business: convention rules; the credentials of delegates; and the party platform, a statement of what the party as a whole stands for. The platform often gives an early indication of which presidential hopeful controls the most delegates, since the platform often reflects the views of the leading candidate.

Then, under the glare of bright television lights from all the major networks, the real business of the convention begins. One by one, prominent supporters nominate their favorite candidates.

A roll call of the states is taken. A spokesperson from each state announces how many delegates are voting in favor of each nominee. The instant the roll call gives one candidate the majority of all possible votes, most of the delegates cheer wildly. The party has nominated a presidential candidate.

Sometimes, no candidate gets a majority of the delegates' votes on the first roll call, and one or more subsequent votes must be taken until someone wins the nomination. When a convention becomes deadlocked in this manner, surprising things can happen. Candidates who never even campaigned for president can be drafted—that is, asked to become a candidate on the spot. In any event, the nomination of a presidential candidate by the party is the highlight of a national convention.

In much the same way, but in less dramatic fashion, the delegates then nominate and vote for a vice presidential candidate. Traditionally, the party's presidential nominee is given a fairly free hand in naming a vice presidential running mate. When both nominees have been selected, the business of the convention is almost over.

Usually, only three months or so separate the end of both national conventions and Election Day in early November. During these months, the campaigns of the Democratic and Republican nominees, as well as those of any third-party candidates strong enough to win a place on many state ballots, become truly national in scope. The candidates may confront one another in televised debates. Heated controversies often arise concerning foreign and domestic issues facing the nation. But the most bitter debates often revolve around the personal qualities of the candidates.

LA ESPERANZA DEL FUTURO

Nuestros hijos merecen una vida
mejor. Regístrese y vote.
SU VOTO ES SU VOZ.

First-time voter (left) receives instructions. Poster (right) encouraging Hispanic-speaking eighteen year olds to register.

As Election Day approaches, the campaign intensity increases.

Since 1845, Congress has specified that presidential Election Day is the first Tuesday after the first Monday in November. On that day, the candidates can finally stop campaigning. For many political workers, however, the day begins long before dawn. Some polls open as early as 6 A.M. local time. Ballots or voting machines and voting booths must be in order. Election officials from the major political parties supervise activities from the time the polling places open in the morning until the votes are counted in the evening.

Until recently, it took many hours to count and report the votes from each polling place. Today, with the help of voting machines, computers, and electronic media, the wait is much shorter. Some polling places can report voting totals, at least in presidential races, within minutes, even seconds, of closing. Poll watchers working for television networks can report the results almost instantly.

During the 1980 elections, ABC, CBS, and NBC all reported that Ronald Reagan had won before many of the polls closed on the West Coast. From the White House, an hour before some people still voted for him in California, President Jimmy Carter publicly admitted he had lost the election. During the 1984 election, the networks withheld their final projections until most polling places had closed.

Sometime during Election Day evening, it is usually clear who will be the next president. The crucial count is the number of electoral votes, as specified in the Constitution, that each candidate has received from the states. However, the formal election is not complete until December, when electors travel to their various state capitols for a brief ceremony in which they cast their votes and sign documents. The president-elect is then sworn in as the new chief executive at a ceremony held in Washington, D.C., at noon on January 20.

Despite a campaign that may have lasted years, the real work of a new president, or of a reelected incumbent, is just beginning. Being president of the United States is an extremely difficult job. When Ronald Reagan knew he had won the 1980 election, he told a story about Abraham Lincoln. When it was clear that Lincoln had won the election of 1860, he gave a brief talk to the newspaper reporters gathered around him. "Well, boys," he said, "your troubles are over now; mine have just begun."

PHOTO CREDITS

AP/Wide World Photos, Inc.—2, 13, 17, 19, 24, 29 (left)
Historical Pictures Service, Chicago—7, 8 (center), 11, 15 (right), 16
    20, 20 (2 photos), 21, 29 (right)
©Norma Morrison—4, 30 (left)
Northwind Picture Archives—10
Photri—1, 18, 27, 32
Roloc Pictorial Research—15 (left), 30 (right)
U.S. Bureau of Printing and Engraving—8 (right and left)

About the Author

   Jim Hargrove has worked as a writer and editor for more than ten years. After serving as an editorial director for three Chicago area publishers, he began a career as an independent writer, preparing a series of books for children. He has contributed to works by nearly twenty different publishers. His Childrens Press titles include biographies of Mark Twain and Richard Nixon. With his wife and daughter, he lives in a small Illinois town near the Wisconsin border.